Japanese Academic Architecture and Seating

For a New Learning Experience

BOOKEND

Japanese Academic Architecture and Seating
For a New Learning Experience

Kotobuki Seating Archive

Seating as an Interface Between Architecture and People
Kazumi Kudo, Architect

In the same way that a chair will summon up an image of a person sitting in it, all furniture can be said to embody human movements or actions and in this respect, it can be said to be anthropomorphic. When designing a building, the concept of the space and the choice of furniture to be installed is decided by the way in which people will move within it. Seating and furniture provide an interface between the space and the human activities that take place there, it has a powerful influence on people's attitude and interaction with the space.

Seating exists to be sat upon and if it consists of sturdy, fixed seats, then the act of sitting is stressed as being the main object of the space. In the University of Tokyo's Yasuda Auditorium, which appears at the beginning of this book, the antique seating causes people to sit up straight and dictates the purpose of the space even more strongly than the surrounding building.

On the other hand, if the seating or furniture can be stored or retracted, it creates a space in which sitting becomes optional. In other words, the development of moveable seating technology has imbued chairs, which are solely for sitting, with flexibility. In recent years, many schools have adopted the concept of multipurpose spaces in which the absence of permanent seating makes it possible for them to be used for various activities other than 'sitting.'

However, the absence of a fixed purpose means that these multipurpose halls tend to be somewhat lacking in 'atmosphere.' For example, a chapel contains such a powerful atmosphere that just to sit inside one brings a feeling a spiritual peace. In a similar way, there are lots of events in the school year—ceremonies, school arts festivals, recitals, etc.—where the students are given the opportunity to take a leading role and rather than simply placing pipe chairs in the gymnasium, a dedicated auditorium with fixed seating, no matter how small, will make them feel much more important. Purpose-specific and multipurpose spaces both have their advantages and disadvantages and in order to decide which to select, it is necessary to focus on what it will be used for.

Recently, I noticed that when I placed a large table, made of wood from Miyazaki Prefecture, inside a university laboratory, the students tended to gather around it. It may suffer a lot of small damage as a result, but this simply provides it with more character. I would like to extend this use of natural materials to chairs and other furniture that is used outdoors. Of course, if they are to be used outside, durability is important, but rather than use tough, easily maintained, manmade materials, a cheap, wooden bench is convenient and easy to use, even though it is prone to decay. Once we accept that damage and decay are characteristics of natural materials, then all that is needed is to replace them regularly.

If this kind of cheap bench were placed in the streets as well as schools, it would provide elderly people with a place to rest while they are out shopping or taking a walk. Today there is a greater choice of materials available than in the past, leading to diversification in both users and applications; chairs or furniture should not be confined to architecture, but rather serve as an interface between local society and people's activities.

This book was published in 2016 by Bookend Publishing Co., Ltd.
in conjunction with the Kotobuki Seating Co., Ltd. 100th anniversary project.
Copyrights © 2016 Kotobuki Seating Co., Ltd.
Book design by Shigeru Orihara
All rights Reserved.
Printed and Bound by Nissha Printing Co., Ltd.
ISBN978-4-907083-36-6

Contents

Section 1 Building the Future on the Past   8
Section 2 Interaction and Communication   78
Section 3 A New Learning Experience   150

List of Works and Photo Credits   236

10	The University of Tokyo ǀ Yasuda Auditorium [Restoration]
16	Chiba University ǀ Inohana Memorial Hall [Restoration]
20	Seijo Gakuen ǀ Sawayanagi Auditorium [Restoration]
24	Seisen University ǀ Main Building, Building No. 1 and No. 2
28	Musashi Academy ǀ Auditorium [Restoration]
32	The Jikei University School of Medicine ǀ The Central Auditorium
36	Waseda University ǀ Okuma Auditorium [Restoration]
40	Yamawaki Gakuen Junior and Senior High School ǀ Yamawaki Hall
44	Waseda University Senior High School ǀ Auditorium
46	Kwansei Gakuin ǀ Central Auditorium
50	Toho Junior and Senior High School ǀ Auditorium, Planetarium
52	Ueno Gakuen ǀ Ishibashi Memorial Hall
56	Kamakura Women's University ǀ Matsumoto Auditorium [Restoration]
58	Tokushima University ǀ Otsuka Memorial University Auditorium [Restoration]
60	Showa Gakuin Junior and Senior High School ǀ Ito Memorial Hall, Main Arena, Planetarium
64	Tokyo Keizai University ǀ Forward Hall [Restoration]
66	Hiroshima University ǀ Satake Memorial Hall
70	Tohoku University ǀ Centennial Hall [Restoration]
72	Kyushu University ǀ Shiiki Hall

1

Building the Future on the Past

The University of Tokyo
Yasuda Auditorium [Restoration]

Location   Tokyo
Architect Chiba Manabu Architects
           Hisao Kohyama Atelier
Completed December 2014

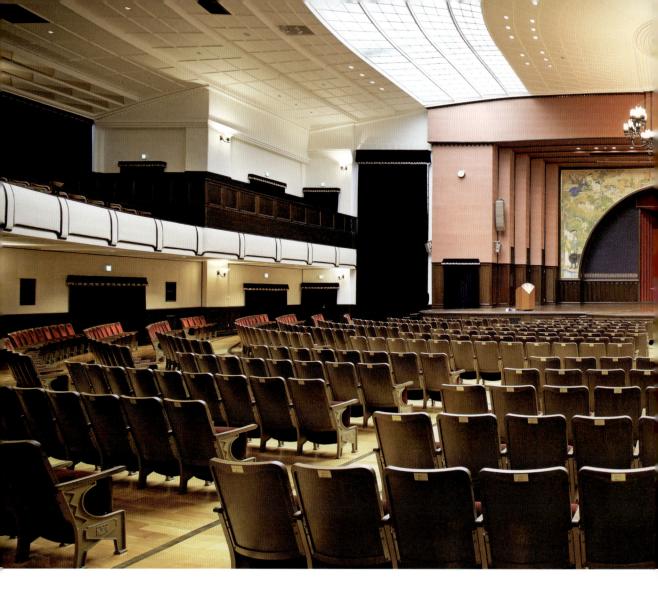

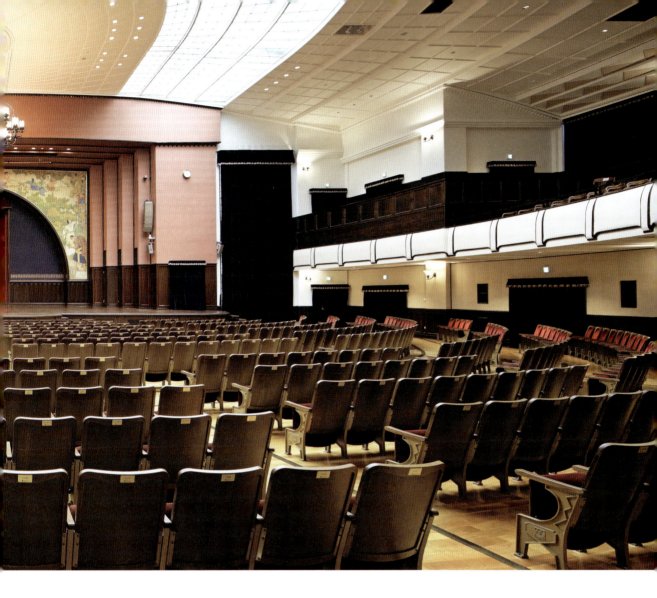

Constructed in 1925, the preliminary design for the Yasuda Auditorium was drawn up by Yoshikazu Uchida (1885–1972), a professor of architecture and later president of the university, with the final design being undertaken by Hideto Kishida (1899–1966). The building has served as a symbol of the university ever since, but after being badly damaged during the student riots of 1968, it was locked up and neglected for over twenty years. The 1980s saw the movement to reopen the auditorium grow, resulting in the 1986 announcement of a plan to restore and preserve the building while respecting its original design. The work was finally carried out in 1990, then, following the Great East Japan Earthquake of 2011, further work was done to reinforce the structure and upgrade the interior. In order to preserve the historical significance of this building as a symbol of the university, every effort was made to restore it to its original appearance.

Restoration, Preservation and Improvement of the Seating During the First Major Repairs
Hisao Kohyama, Architect

Work began on a major improvement project in 1989. This is now referred to as the 'First Major Heisei Restoration.' The interior of the auditorium had been partially destroyed during the student protests while the entrance lobby and Emperor's anteroom were wrecked when the police carried out a frontal assault on the building. Chairs had been broken to be used as barricades, the wooden floors were ripped up and burnt and the marble fittings in the lobby disappeared after being smashed to provide rocks to throw at the police.... Plans were drawn up for the restoration/preservation of the edifice with necessary improvements carried out wherever possible, these were approved and work began smoothly....Although the main objective was the preservation/restoration of the building, two major changes were made to the interior—one being the number of seats and the other the shape of the rostrum. The original rostrum had been designed for outmoded events and was not suitable for modern ceremonies, symposiums, etc., so it was decided that it should be completely rebuilt. However, the seating harmonized beautifully with the design of the interior and so every effort was made to preserve it. Kotobuki Seating, which was the first company to manufacture lecture-room furniture in Japan and whose founder was a friend of the Auditorium's original architect, Yoshikazu Uchida, took the design of the original, damaged seats, enlarged it to suit the improved physique of today's students and added a modern mechanism. As a result of the increased size, the total number of seats dropped by one third, from 1,738 to 1,144, but this is more suitable to an auditorium of this scale.

Plan for restoration of Yasuda Auditorium showing the eastern elevation.
Drawing: Toshikazu Kawai. Courtesy of the Hisao Kohyama Atelier

Chiba University
Inohana Memorial Hall [Restoration]

Built in 1963 to mark the 85th anniversary of the establishment of the university's Medical Department, the architect Fumihiko Maki (1928–) based this innovative building, with its undressed concrete walls and copper roof, on the image of a Shinto shrine standing in a sacred grove. Having stood for approximately 50 years, it was decided to renovate the building and in addition to general maintenance and earthquake proofing, the sound absorption/insulation was improved, the stage and acoustic facilities upgraded and the interior and stage refurbished. First floor seating was reduced from 720 to 576, providing more space while also providing accommodation for wheelchairs.

Location   Chiba
Architect Maki and Associates
Completed April 2014

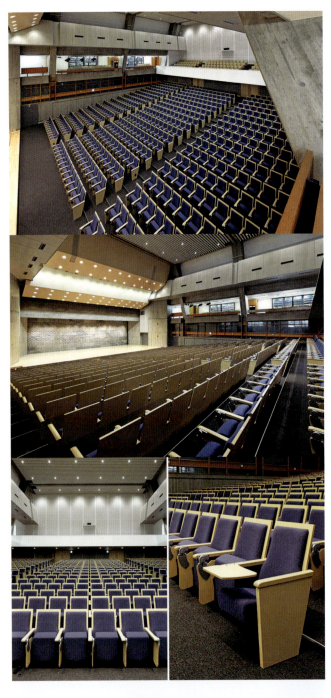

Suggesting the Image of a Shrine in a Sacred Grove

Hirochika Kashima, Maki and Associates

This facility was constructed in 1963 to celebrate the 85th anniversary of the establishment of the Medical Department and was the 2nd such structure in Japan to be designed by Fumihiko Maki after Nagoya University's Toyoda Auditorium. The university's Medical Department began with a hospital established in 1874 using funds donated by the local people then in 1890 it moved to its present site in Inohanadai. This was the site of Inohana Castle, built by the Chiba clan in the 12th century and seven tumuli, known as the 'Shichi tennozuka', still remain there. Acting as a commemorative symbol expressing respect to the location's history, the open trapezoid cross-section of the front, that looks out over an open space, is suggestive of the image of a shrine standing in a sacred grove. With a sloping roof in copper and an undressed, molded concrete exterior, the interior provides a large, relaxed space.

In 2014 it was decided that, due to general wear and tear and the necessity of strengthening major buildings after the great earthquake of 2011, the hall should undergo renovation. The main objectives were: the reinforcement of the building to help it withstand earthquakes, the renovation of the exterior and its undressed concrete finish, improvement of weatherproofing, removal of asbestos from the interior, the improvement of all the facilities, the upgrade of the hall's functions and sound absorption/insulation, enhancement of the stage acoustics, renovation of the interior and stage, and the renewal of the louvered ceiling. The number of seats on the first floor was reduced from 720 to 576 to provide seats that were of a better suited to the improved physique of today's young people and each was fitted with a memo table.

A steel and concrete mural by Masayuki Nagare creates a marvelous fusion of architecture and art (p. 19, top) and possesses a great sense of presence. This renovation project received a commendation at the 25th BELCA (Building and Equipment Long-Life Cycle Association) Awards for the effort displayed in retaining the essence of this fifty-year-old building while upgrading its overall function.

Seijo Gakuen
Sawayanagi Auditorium [Restoration]

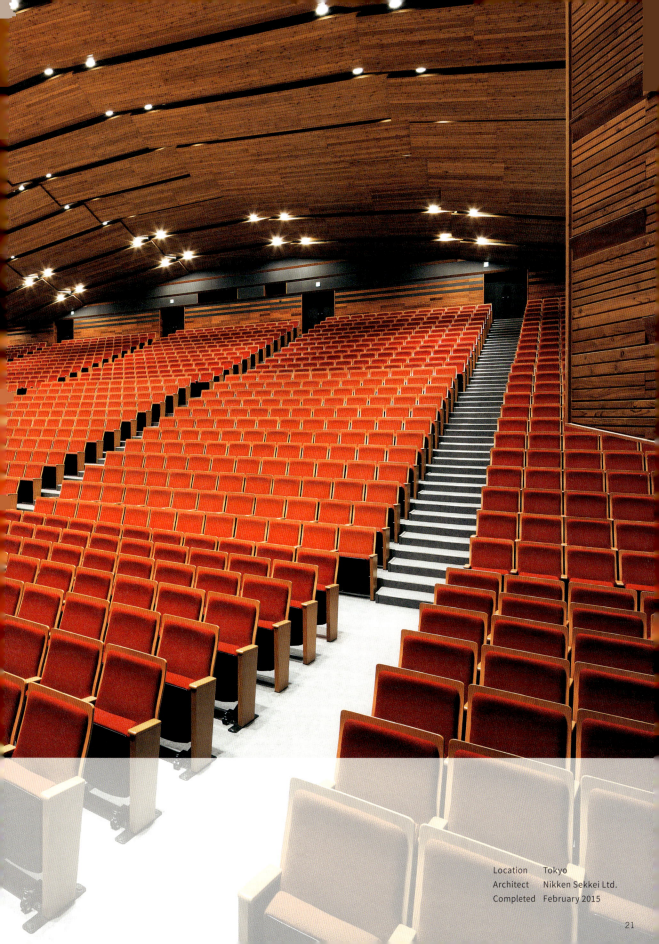

Location   Tokyo
Architect Nikken Sekkei Ltd.
Completed February 2015

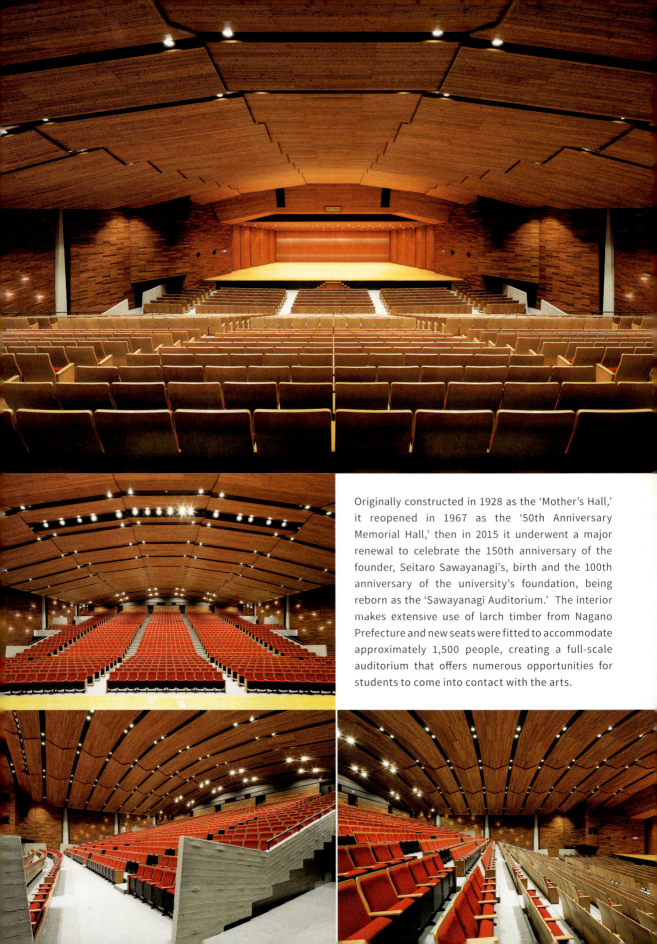

Originally constructed in 1928 as the 'Mother's Hall,' it reopened in 1967 as the '50th Anniversary Memorial Hall,' then in 2015 it underwent a major renewal to celebrate the 150th anniversary of the founder, Seitaro Sawayanagi's, birth and the 100th anniversary of the university's foundation, being reborn as the 'Sawayanagi Auditorium.' The interior makes extensive use of larch timber from Nagano Prefecture and new seats were fitted to accommodate approximately 1,500 people, creating a full-scale auditorium that offers numerous opportunities for students to come into contact with the arts.

Seisen University
Main Building, Building No. 1 and No. 2

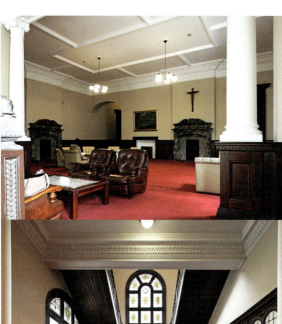

Building No. 1 and No. 2

Location   Tokyo
Architect   Mitsubishi Jisho Sekkei Inc.
            Takenaka Corporation
Completed   September 2013

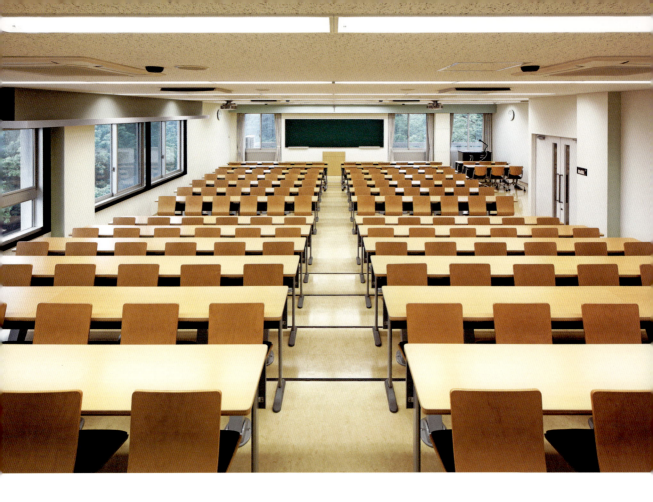

This renaissance-style Main Building (pp. 24-25, 27) that has become the school's symbol, was designed by the British architect Josiah Conder (1852–1920) as the home of Prince Tadashige Shimazu and constructed in 1915. With a hand-carved marble fireplace, ionic columns and great staircase, it is of great historical value and in 2012 it was designated an important cultural property by the Tokyo Metropolitan Government. The stained glass in the building all dates back to its original construction in 1915 and presents symmetrical designs in the *art nouveau*-style. The second floor, which used to house bedrooms for the prince, princess and children, has been converted into classrooms and a conference room.

In contrast to the Main Building, Buildings No. 1 and No. 2 (p. 26), which were refurbished between 2011–13, have numerous large windows, creating an open atmosphere. In addition to large classrooms (top) and multipurpose spaces, they also contain a cafeteria, a shop, the student hall, etc., providing all the facilities necessary for campus life.

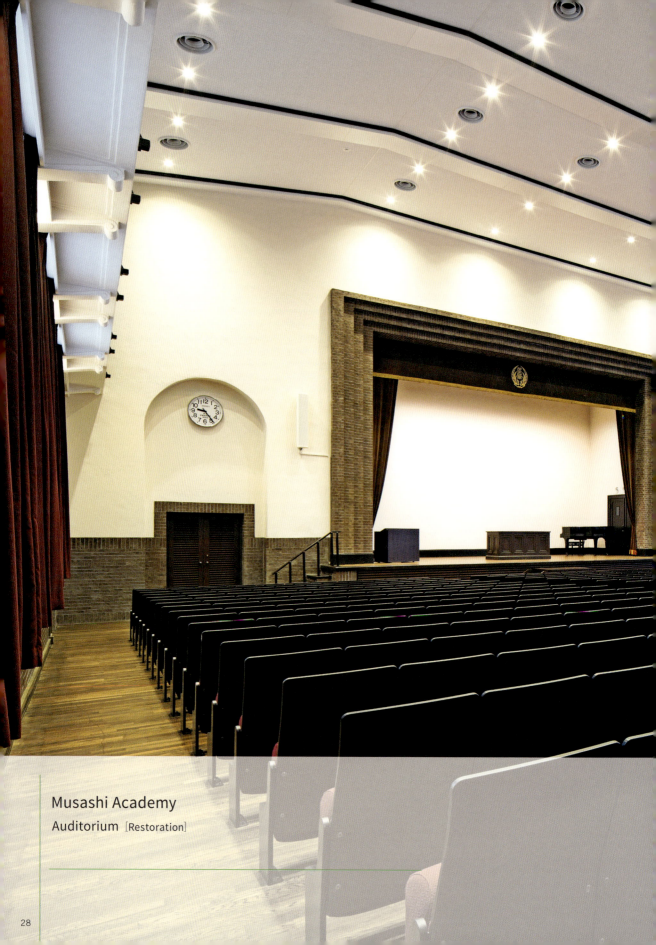

Musashi Academy
Auditorium [Restoration]

Location	Tokyo
Architect	Shimizu Corporation
Completed	October 2011

With a history extending over 90 years, the Ekoda campus contains numerous well-tended, large trees, which together with the Susugigawa River that runs through the center of the grounds, create a rich, bucolic space. Comprising of a junior high school, senior high school and university, it is situated within 60,000 square meters of land and the school buildings, that were built at different periods for different purposes, harmonize with the natural surroundings to create a tranquil setting.

    The Great Lecture Hall, which was constructed in 1928, was designed by Koichi Sato (1878–1941) who also designed the Okuma Memorial Hall (Waseda University) and the Tokyo Metropolitan Hibiya Public Hall. This two-story building employs a combination of reinforced concrete and steel construction, retaining a gothic style overall, while introducing *modernisme* into its decoration. The exterior tiles, windows, roof and ceiling, etc., were restored to the original design and even now, 90 years after it was first constructed, it retains the atmosphere of that period. Its continued maintenance over such a long period has won recognition with Building No. 3, together with the Musashi University's Nezu Chemical Institute, winning the 25th BELCA (Sustainable Architecture) Award. Currently, the Great Lecture Hall is used for the entrance and graduation ceremonies while the exhibition space on the second floor holds a display featuring the school's history.

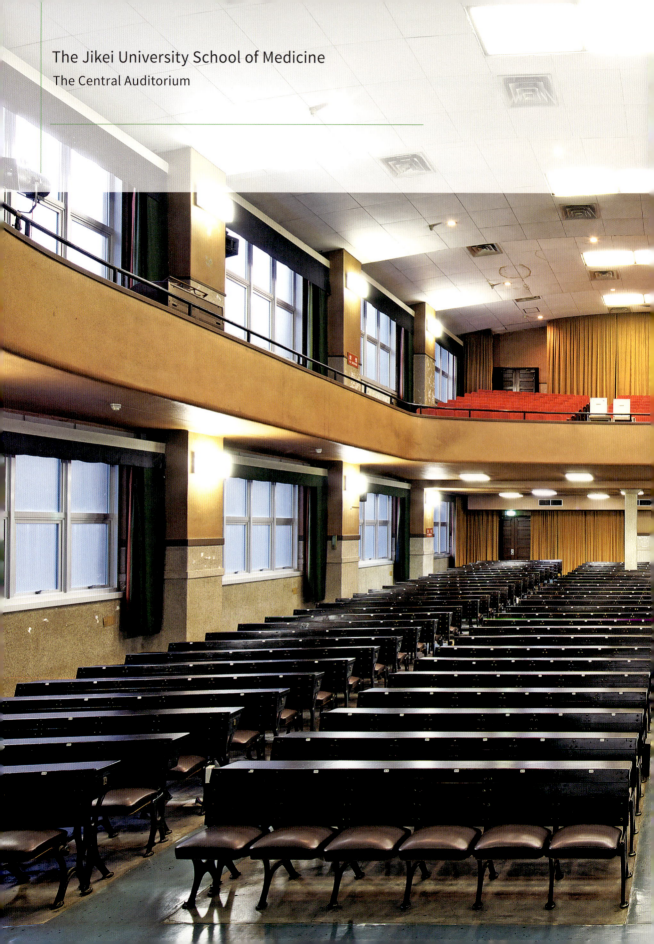

The Jikei University School of Medicine
The Central Auditorium

Location Tokyo
Architect Shigeharu Nomura,
　　　　　Makoto Akaishi,
　　　　　Seiichiro Okumura
Completed December 1932

With its roots reaching back to the Sei-i-kai medical society that was founded in 1881, this is Japan's oldest, private medical school and has a history extending for over 130 years. The university and its affiliated hospital were destroyed in the fires that followed the Great Kanto Earthquake of 1923 and part of the hospital was destroyed again during the 1945 bombing of Tokyo, but despite this, a modern hospital building dating back to the prewar years still remains in the campus. The main university building was designed by Shigeharu Nomura and constructed in 1932. The desks and chairs in the central auditorium date back to this time and have provided a learning space for 80 years. During the renovation, the desk legs, which are engraved with the school insignia, the wooden backrests and the desktops were all repaired, while the leather cushions were reupholstered by skilled craftsmen, maintaining the dignified atmosphere of the space.

Waseda University
Okuma Auditorium [Restoration]

Location	Tokyo
Architect	AXS Satow Inc.
Completed	October 2007

Completed in 1927, this building, which serves as the university's symbol, was designed and built by Koichi Sato (1878–1941) and Takeo Sato (1899–1972). In 2007, the building was restored/reincarnated as a multipurpose cultural hall. The scratch tiles that cover the exterior walls of this gothic structure were badly deteriorated and the majority of them had to be removed and restored. In the interior, the beautiful ceiling and other fittings of the auditorium were restored and preserved while the structure was strengthened to make it earthquake resistant; air conditioning, IT facilities and the latest audiovisual equipment were also installed. In addition, work was carried out to make the building barrier free and provide facilities for wheelchair users.

Yamawaki Gakuen Junior and Senior High School
Yamawaki Hall

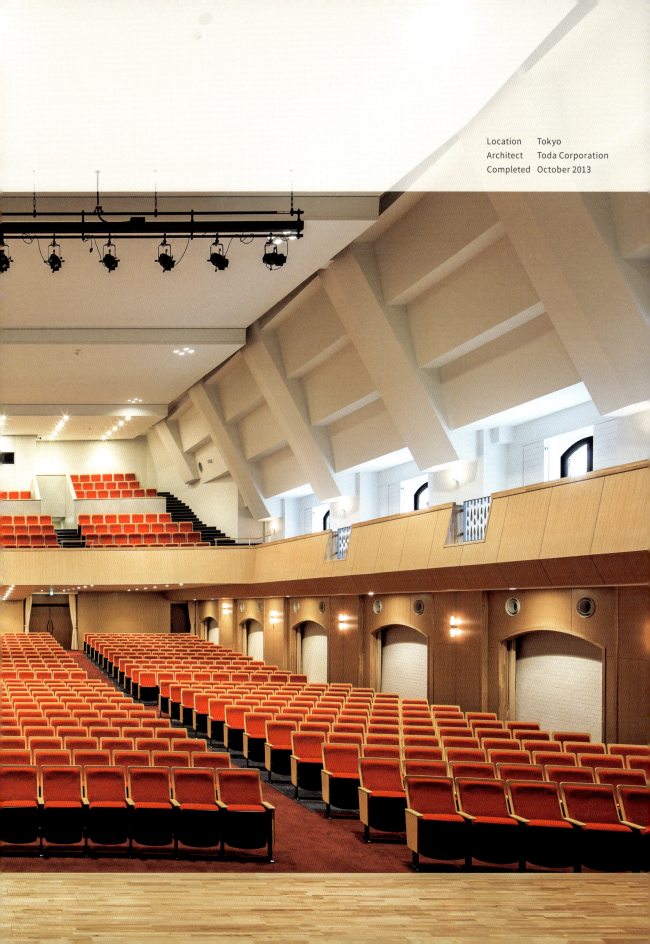

Location   Tokyo
Architect   Toda Corporation
Completed   October 2013

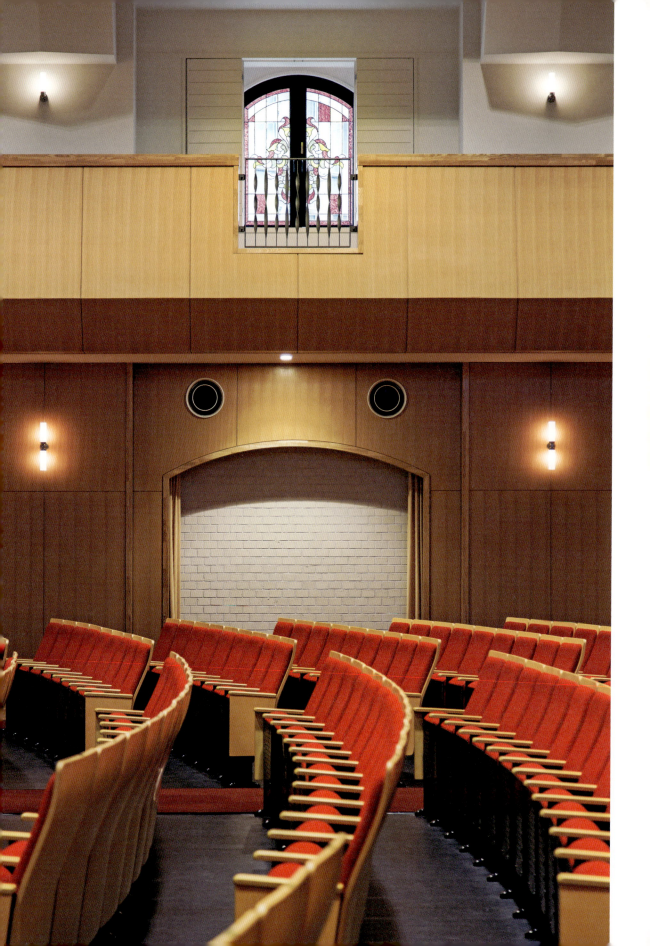

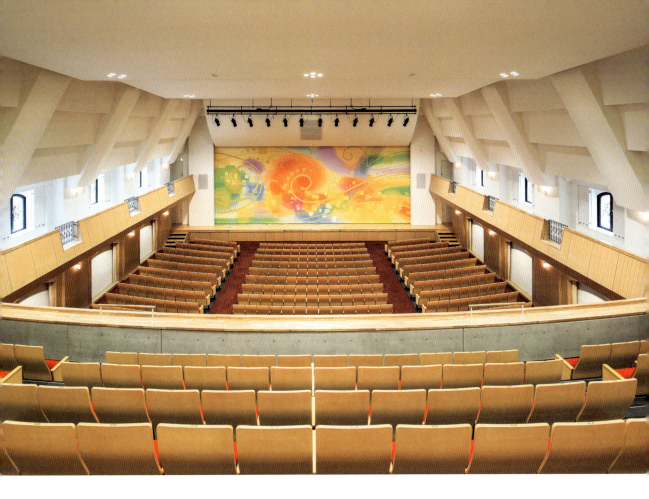

Founded as a girl's school in 1903, Yamawaki Gakuen celebrated its centenary in 2003. In what has been described as the 'Yamawaki Renaissance' the old junior college facilities were converted into a combined junior and senior high school in 2009 with the aim of creating a new style of education. The school buildings were replaced or renewed, while unique learning facilities and programs for languages and the natural sciences were introduced to create an innovative educational environment. In 2013 work was completed on a new school building. The auditorium, which is named Yamawaki Hall, is characterized by the light-colored wood interior, a flamboyant drop curtain, stained glass windows, and seating finished in orange upholstery. Capable of holding 900, it is used for a wide variety of events including ceremonies, recitals, musical concerts etc.

Waseda University Senior High School
Auditorium

Location   Tokyo
Architect Nikken Sekkei Ltd.
Completed March 2014

The auditorium complex, which was built in 2014, combines a lecture hall capable of seating 1,508, with a music room and music related facilities. The interior walls consist entirely of concrete and have panels that have been fitted at varying angles to improve the acoustics.

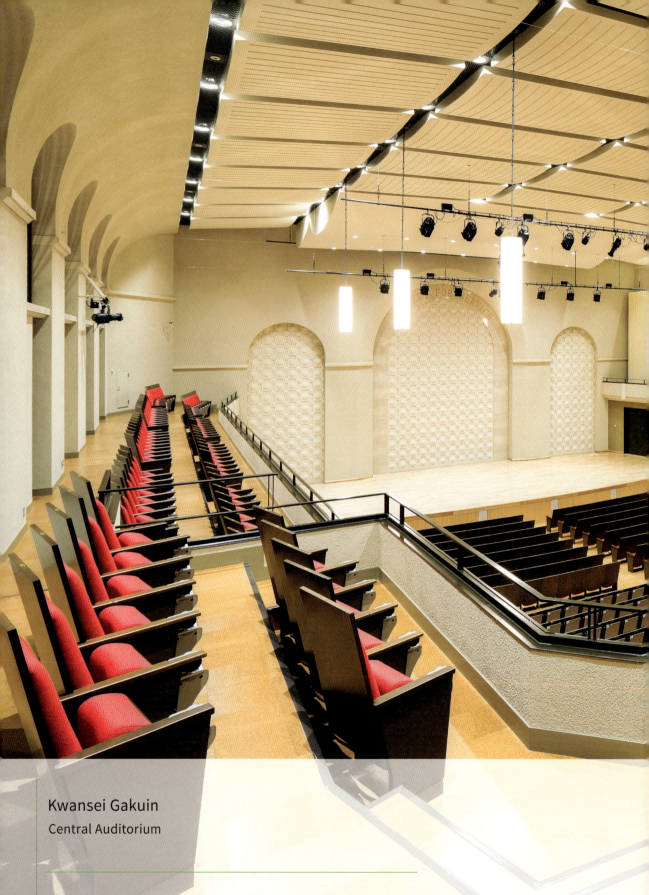

Kwansei Gakuin
Central Auditorium

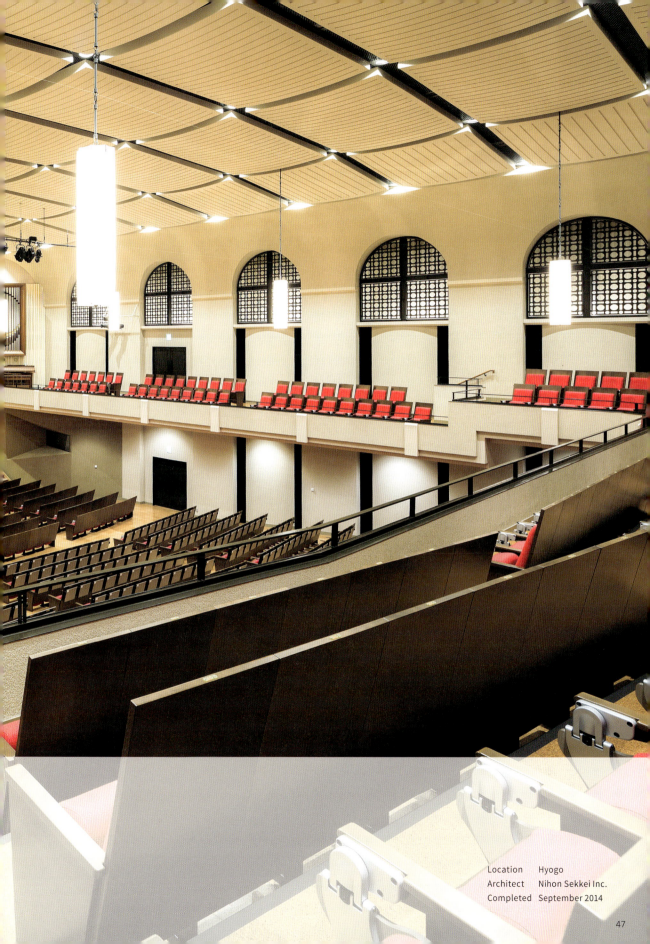

Location	Hyogo
Architect	Nihon Sekkei Inc.
Completed	September 2014

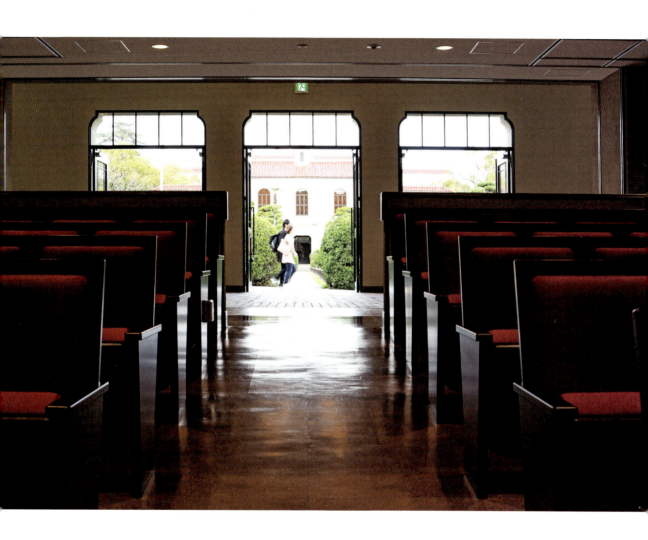

The building with the red-tiled roof facing the central lawn preserves the exterior appearance of the old central auditorium that was designed by William Merrell Vories (1880–1964). The first and second floors of this hall are capable of seating a total of 1,200. The front four rows of seats can be raised or lowered and the size of the stage altered as required, providing space to hold anything up to a Romantic orchestra.

The hall boasts a pipe organ, made by the Austrian company, Rieger, and is also fitted with a simultaneous translation booth, allowing it to be utilized for a wide variety of events, from international symposiums to religious services. Donations were gathered to pay for the 125th Anniversary work and a message of gratitude, together with the names of the donors is inscribed on the seats.

Toho Junior and Senior High School
Auditorium, Planetarium

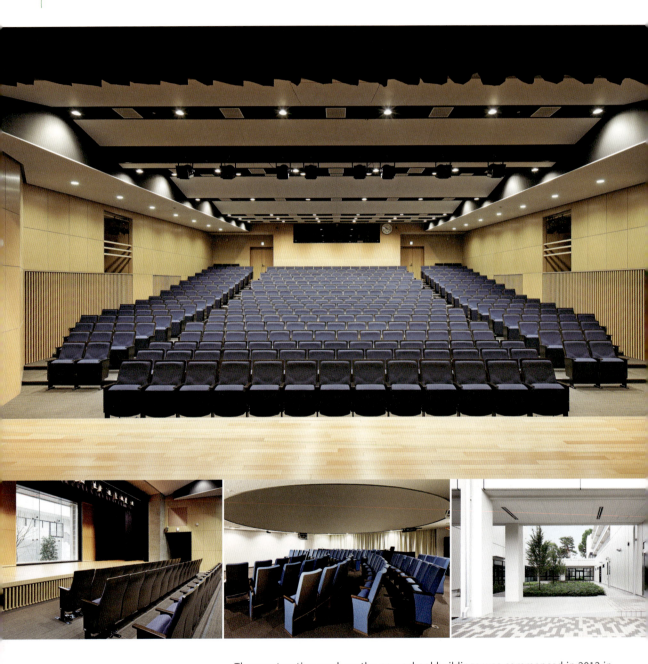

Location: Tokyo
Architect: Yamashita Sekkei Inc.
Completed: June 2014

The construction work on the new school buildings was commenced in 2012 in preparation for the school's 75th anniversary in 2016. 2013 saw the completion of the new classroom building that also includes a planetarium. The new hall, which was completed in 2014, has a unique design with a glassed-in area in the front that allows the daylight to flood in when the doors are opened.

Ueno Gakuen
Ishibashi Memorial Hall

The school's old auditorium, the Ishibashi Memorial Hall that was constructed in 1974 to celebrate the school's 70th anniversary, was rebuilt. Including the seats on the balcony, it is capable of seating 508. The pipe organ from the old hall, which was made by Germany's Johannes Klais Orgelbau, was reinstalled and despite retaining the same basic shape of the ceiling and walls around the stage area (shoebox-style), the new facility succeeds in improving on the excellent acoustics of the old hall. In order to reduce vibration, a floating floor was fitted, creating a musical space that can even be used for recordings. In order to facilitate orchestral concerts, the width and depth of the stage were enlarged. Seating for parents to watch with their children is available to the rear of the audience seats (bottom left).

Location   Tokyo
Architect   Atelier Platform for Architectural Design
            GKK Architects & Engineers Co., Ltd.
Completed   February 2009

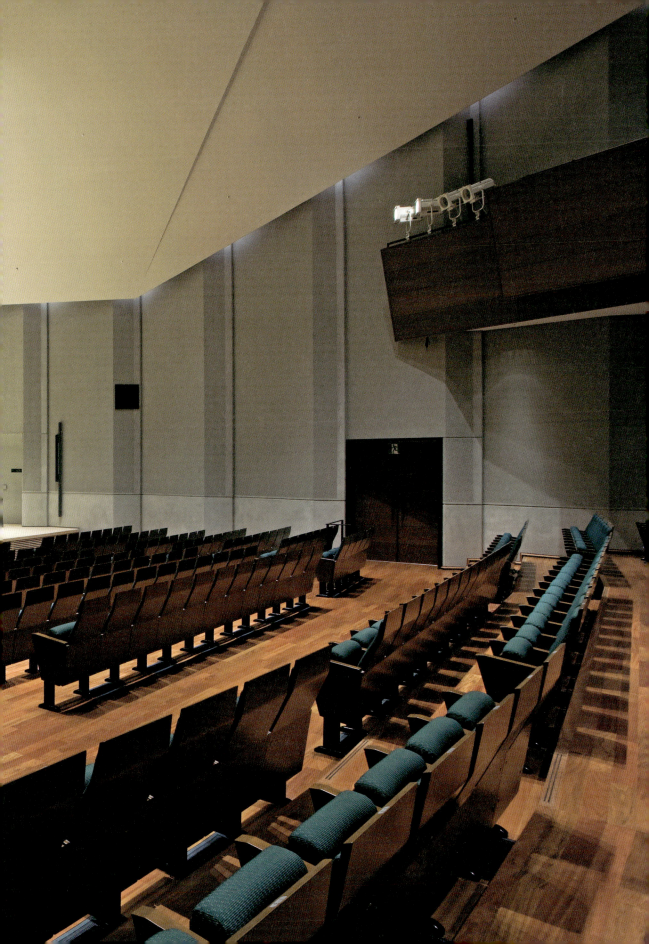

Kamakura Women's University
Matsumoto Auditorium [Restoration]

Location Kanagawa
Architect Shimizu Corporation
Completed March 2014

All the buildings on the Iwase Campus, from kindergarten to senior high school were renovated in 2003. In 2004 a Japanese archery range and an indoor swimming pool (that won the Award for Excellence and Appeal Award), were added. The Auditorium, which is capable of holding 1,300, serves as a symbol of the university and is used for various ceremonies, lectures, choral concerts, etc. When renovations, including the installation of an earthquake-proof reinforced ceiling, were carried out in 2013, the characteristic red tone of the seats, which have tables fitted into their backs, was retained.

Tokushima University
Otsuka Memorial University Auditorium [Restoration]

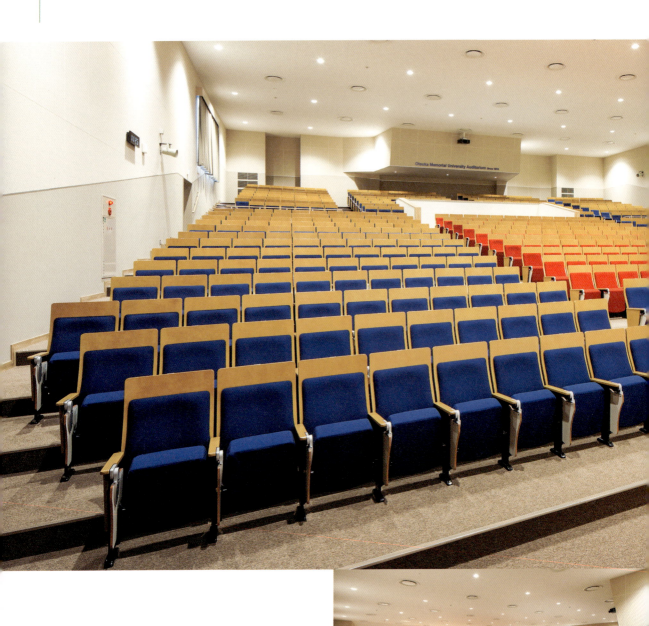

Location   Tokushima
Architect   Takimoto Architect & Associates
Completed   April 2013

Built in 1965, this auditorium has hosted numerous ceremonies and symposiums. During the renovation work in 2013, the windows were enlarged, letting in more daylight and creating a bright, airy atmosphere. The large hall has seating for 655 and space for 18 wheelchairs while 2 small halls were also added to provide space for lectures and practical teaching. Moreover, when lectures are being held in the large hall, it is possible to watch the events on screens in the small halls, facilitating its use for conferences and other extramural activities.

Showa Gakuin Junior and Senior High School
Ito Memorial Hall, Main Arena, Planetarium

In celebration of its 70th anniversary, a general renovation of the entire school complex was initiated. The Ito Memorial Hall, that was completed in 2009, has become the new symbol of the campus. Capable of holding 560, the hall also has an annex containing a museum depicting the school's history. Supported by precast, folded-plate beams, this large structure not only presents an impressive appearance, but is also outstanding both structurally and acoustically. In 2010 an arena and indoor swimming pool were also completed. The main arena is fitted with electrically-powered, moveable seating allowing the space to be tailored to suit a wide range of sports events and ceremonies. There is also a planetarium on the fourth floor of the school building.

Location   Chiba
Architect Nikken Sekkei Ltd.
Completed May 2010

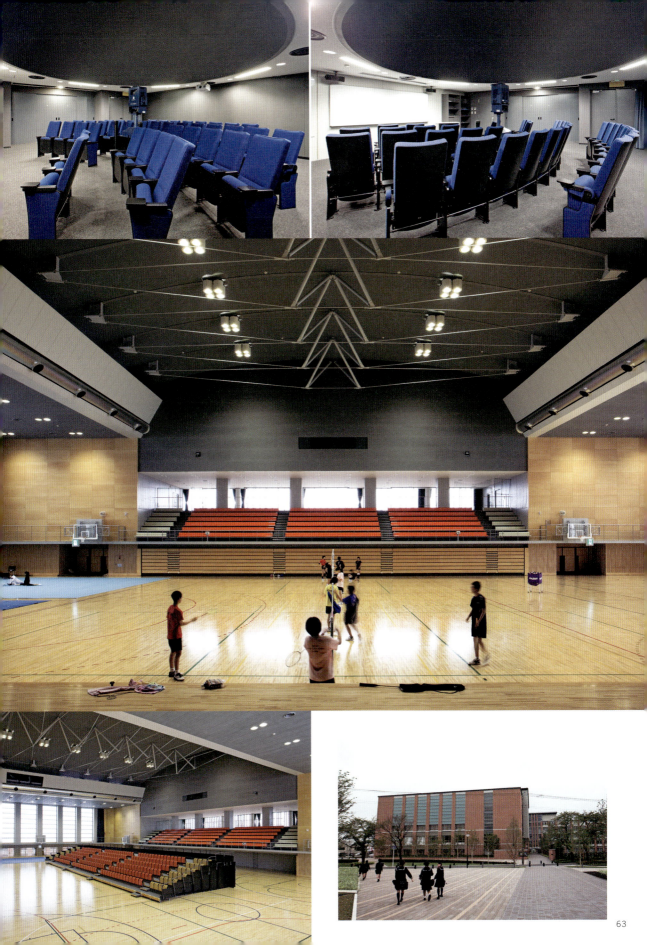

Tokyo Keizai University
Forward Hall [Restoration]

Location   Tokyo
Architect AXS Satow Inc.
Completed October 2014

Work was undertaken in 2014 to renovate the library building that was designed by Azusa Kito (1926–2008) and built in 1968. With windows fitted into all four walls, allowing it to meld into the surrounding forest, the huge open space on the 1st floor was converted into a multipurpose hall with seating for 320 and an area set aside for history exhibits. The hall is separated from the foyer and gallery by a glass wall, not only allowing the entire area to be used integrally but also offering a view of the forest behind the stage, creating a natural backdrop for musical performances or lectures. The basement contains the office of the alumni association, a lounge for graduates, a conference room, etc.

Hiroshima University
Satake Memorial Hall

Location   Hiroshima
Architect   Taisei Corporation
Completed   February 2003

Begun in 1999 as part of the university's 50th anniversary celebrations, construction was completed in 2003. The exterior design is based on the image of a grand piano keyboard. This unique, hexagonal hall employs a large amount of wood in its interior, the stage comprises of solid cherry boards, the walls surrounding the seating area are of oak and the floor is beech, giving rise to a unique acoustic effect. Capable of holding 1,000 the hall is open to the local people and is used for dramatic performances, local medical forums, etc.

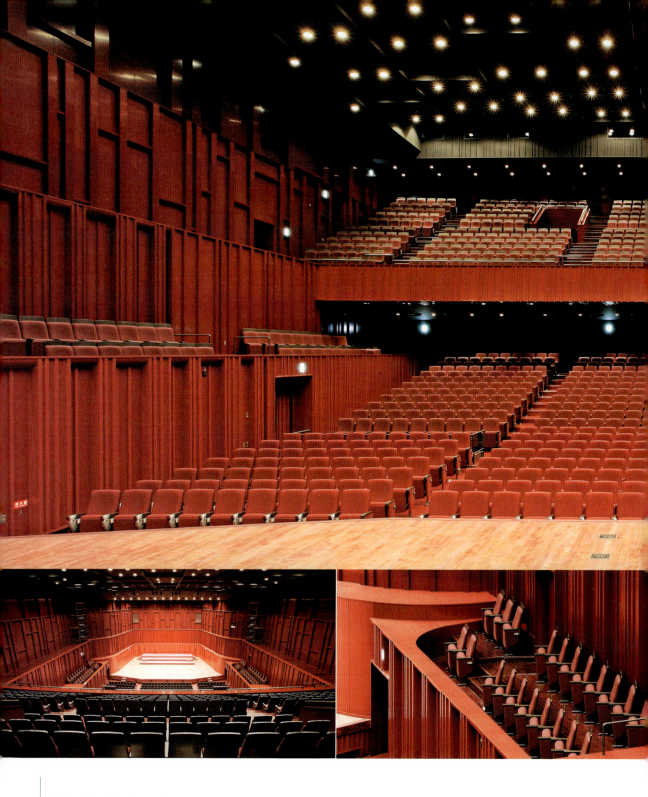

Tohoku University
Centennial Hall [Restoration]

Built in 1960, this hall underwent a major restoration as part of the university's centennial anniversary celebrations. The 50-year-old exterior design was preserved as much as possible while in contrast, the interior was upgraded using the latest facilities and an individualistic design. Hitoshi Abe, who is a graduate and also the Chair of the UCLA Department of Architecture and Urban Design, was commissioned to produce the basic concept and supervise the design. The hall's acoustics were handled by the Yoichi Suzuki Laboratory of the university's Research Institute of Electronic Communication, producing an environment suitable as both a concert hall and an international conferences venue.

Location   Miyagi
Architect Mitsubishi Jisho Sekkei Inc.
Completed August 2008

Kyushu University
Shiiki Hall

Based on the dark red school color, the seats in the hall are upholstered in a fabric that employs wine-red threads in warp and black threads in the weft to create a waffle weave. The texture and luster that this creates imbues the whole space with a sense of depth. The rear of the hall can be cut off using soundproofed walling, to provide a conference or lecture room.

Set within a circular building, 100 meters in diameter, this complex was constructed to celebrate the university's centenary and contains both the main concert hall and an administrative section. Capable of seating 3,000, the concert hall is used for university ceremonies, conferences and other large events. In addition, the auditorium also contains the semicircular Galleria open space, (top), a large conference room, a permanent display gallery and exhibition space, and a restaurant. Its doors are open to conferences, lectures and exhibitions from outside the university.

Location   Fukuoka
Architect   Naito Architect & Associates
Completed   March 2014

80	Shikoku Gakuin University	Notos Studio
86	Bunkyo University Junior and Senior High School	Lotus Hall
90	Toin University of Yokohama | Central Tower, Creative Studio, Auditorium
94	Meguro Seibi Gakuen Junior and Senior High School
98	Rissho University	Dining Hall No. 2 [Restoration]
102	Suijo High School	Yamanouchi Hall
106	Kansai University Hokuyo Junior and Senior High School | Gymnasium
110	Kaichi Nihonbashi Gakuen Junior High School/ Nihonbashi Jogakkan High School	Multipurpose Hall
112	Hongo Junior and Senior High School	Auditorium
114	Yasuda Gakuen Junior and Senior High School | Communication Spaces
118	The American School in Japan	Multi-Purpose Room
120	Polaris College of Nursing	Megrez Hall
124	Kyoto Sangyo University	Musubiwaza Hall
128	Kawasaki Junior and Senior High School	Auditorium
132	Toyama Chubu High School	Shisei Hall
134	Kyushu High School Affiliated with Kyushu Sangyo University | Kyushu Community Hall
136	Shoshikan High School	Audiovisual Hall
138	Nakano Junior and Senior High School Attached to Meiji University | Sakurayama Hall
140	Hokkaido Otani Muroran High School	Auditorium
142	Nichinan Gakuen Junior and Senior High School	Portsmouth Hall
144	Tamagawa University	Drama Studio
146	Aoyama Gakuin Elementary School	Yoneyama Memorial Chapel

2

Interaction and Communication

Shikoku Gakuin University
Notos Studio

The Notos Studio, which is housed on the 1st floor of new building that was constructed on the southern side of the campus in 2006, is used regularly for theatrical and dance performances by both students and professionals. It can be used as an open-floor facility for basic practice sessions but also contains moveable seating that can be brought out or stored by the students according to their needs. It served as the venue for the Shikoku High School Drama Summit and as it is open to the local residents, it also plays an important role as a communication space.

A Local Center for Cultural Exchange
Kazuhiro Nishimura, Notos Studio Artistic Director

The first formal drama course in the Chugoku/Shikoku area was established in 2011 at Shikoku Gakuin University. The dramatist and director, Oriza Hirata, was invited to act as special advisor to the president and among the lecturers are numerous directors and choreographers who are active at the forefront of the theatrical world. It offers a revolutionary program that has been well-received from the outset and has achieved great results, including being invited to participate in the official program for the Setouchi Triennale in 2013.

Central to its activities is the Notos Studio, a small theater capable of holding approximately 80 people, where students act as both staff and cast to present theatrical performances. It is used to hold numerous small-scale performances or study groups, offering drama and dance workshops aimed at local children up to high school age and as a venue for performances by professional theater groups who are invited to visit from Tokyo. These performances and workshops have proved very popular, attracting more people as the program progresses and it can be said that this is because the Notos Studio functions as a 'local theater.'

In the future it is hoped to present more workshops, plays and original dramas with the participation of the local citizens, offering the people greater opportunity to involve themselves in the production. The aim is to make it more accessible, creating a theater that functions as a local center for social interaction, while simultaneously inspiring the people who will become leaders of the local culture and artistic activities. In addition it will work closely with the Sunport Hall Takamatsu, the Museum of Art, Kochi and other public halls or museums, to promote culture and art in Shikoku, building a diverse and attractive society that will encourage young people live there.

Location   Kagawa
Architect   Showa Sekkei, Incorporated
Completed   May 2006

Bunkyo University Junior and Senior High School
Lotus Hall

Location	Tokyo
Architect	Nihon Sekkei Inc.
Completed	April 2014

The concept behind the planning of the new school buildings for this school was that of 'ports.' The building that deals with school's central functions is known as the 'Mother Port' while the other four buildings are named according to their position in relation to this. The 'West Port,' which resembles a bows of a ship, was completed in 2014 and houses the junior high school. The hall that is located in the basement and first floor of this building takes its name from the school's emblem, the lotus. It is characterized by the arch-like beams that support the ceiling and resemble the ribs of a ship's hull. The illumination has been positioned to create bright arcs of light. Deploying both the moveable seating and stacking chairs, it is possible to seat 700, but all of this may be moved into storage to create an open space.

A Space to Provide a Ray of Hope for the Future
Shinjiro Inoue, Nihon Sekkei Inc.

These school buildings house the students from junior to senior high school, a period of six years during which the students undergo various changes, and thought was given to provide them with the facilities they need at this time. It has been laid out so the 'West Port' houses the junior high school, the 'East Port' houses the senior high school and the central 'Mother Port' contains a 'learning center,' comprising of the library, special classrooms and staff room. Each building has work spaces scattered throughout and are provided with places for communication. It was hoped that each workspace could also serve as an area where the students could interact with each other. The 'West Port' houses the junior high school; the 2nd to 4th floors form a dedicated school zone while the basement and 1st floor house the auditorium, the 'Lotus Hall.' Structural arches placed at 2.8-meter intervals transmit the weight of upper three stories into the surrounding ground, making it possible to create a large underground space. This row of white arches supports the structure while soft illumination, provided by high sidelights, produces a space combining gentleness and dignity.

Toin University of Yokohama
Central Tower, Creative Studio, Auditorium

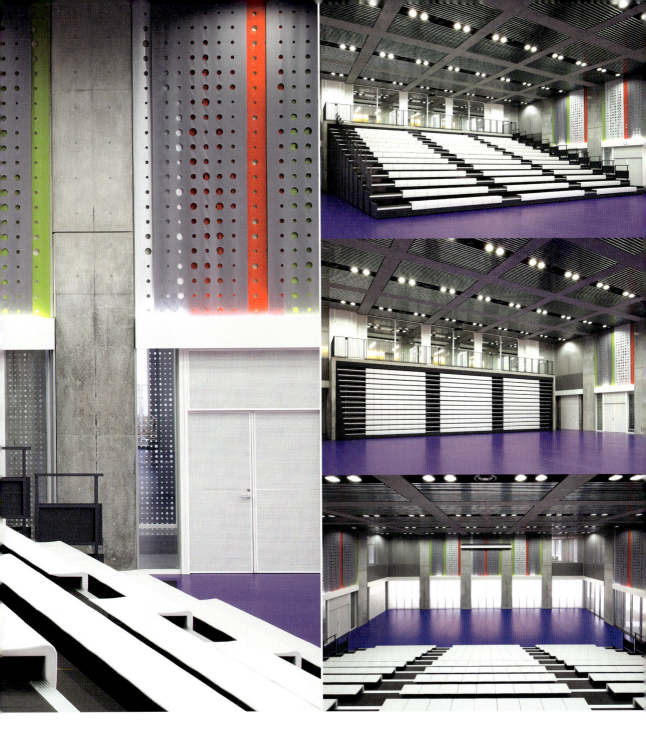

Location   Kanagawa
Architect   Shimizu Corporation
Completed   March 2010

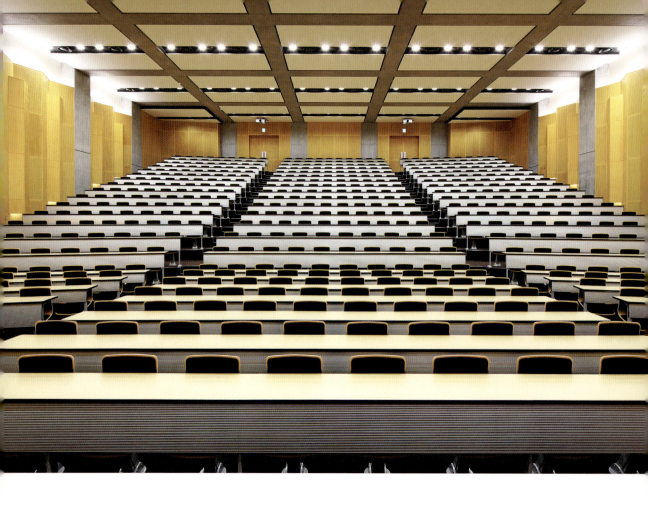

The glass-clad Central Tower has a powerful presence in the campus. Containing an auditorium capable of seating 600, it also provides a large variety of study spaces. Among these is the Creative Studio, in which the unfinished concrete walls, combined with the bold use of color, produce a modern design. The electrically powered moveable seating can be deployed to produce a tiered audience area or moved back against the wall to provide a space for creative learning and practical lectures.

Meguro Seibi Gakuen Junior and Senior High School

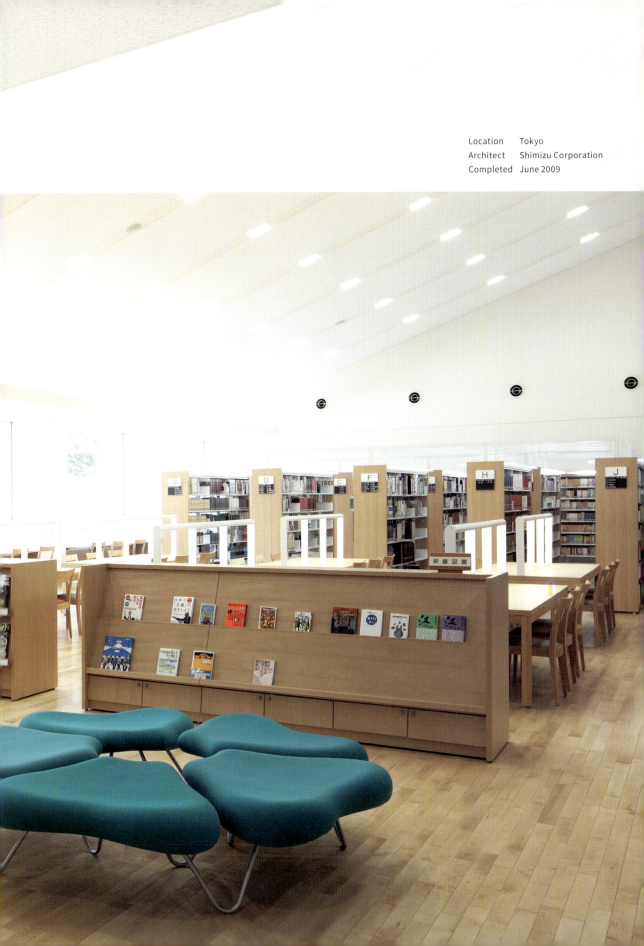

Location   Tokyo
Architect   Shimizu Corporation
Completed   June 2009

Meguro Seibi Gakuen is a mission school that offers a comprehensive 6-year educational course. It was decided to improve the facilities as part of the 50th anniversary celebrations of the school's establishment and this was achieved by constructing a new L-shaped building overlooking the natural grass sports ground. In addition to ordinary classrooms, the building contains a biology laboratory and other special purpose rooms, all of which are connected by lounges containing tables and chairs. The open library shares the same concept of providing a place where students can interact with each other (p. 94) while the Maria Hall (top right), with its tiered auditorium seating, provides a interior design that is ideally suited to a girls' school.

Rissho University
Dining Hall No. 2 [Restoration]

Location   Tokyo
Architect Maeda Corporation
Completed June 2014

Rissho University can trace its roots back to the Iidaka Danrin, an educational institution founded in 1580 to teach priests belonging to the Nichiren sect of Buddhism, and even in its present form, it celebrated its 140th anniversary in 2012. In 2013 its affiliated junior and senior high schools moved to Nishi-Magome in Tokyo's Ota Ward and work was begun to redevelop their old site. In addition to creating a 'student square,' planted with trees and fitted with benches, Dining Hall No. 2 opened on the second floor of Building No. 7 in 2014. Fitted with skylights to provide natural lighting, this large columnless space offers seating for over 300, providing nutritious, balanced meals and freshly-baked bread to support the students' eating habits. Outside of meal times, it offers drinks, deserts and other snacks. The tables and chairs can be moved, allowing the layout to be changed freely. Its use is not confined to dining; it can also be used for receptions, briefings and other purposes to promote interchange among the students.

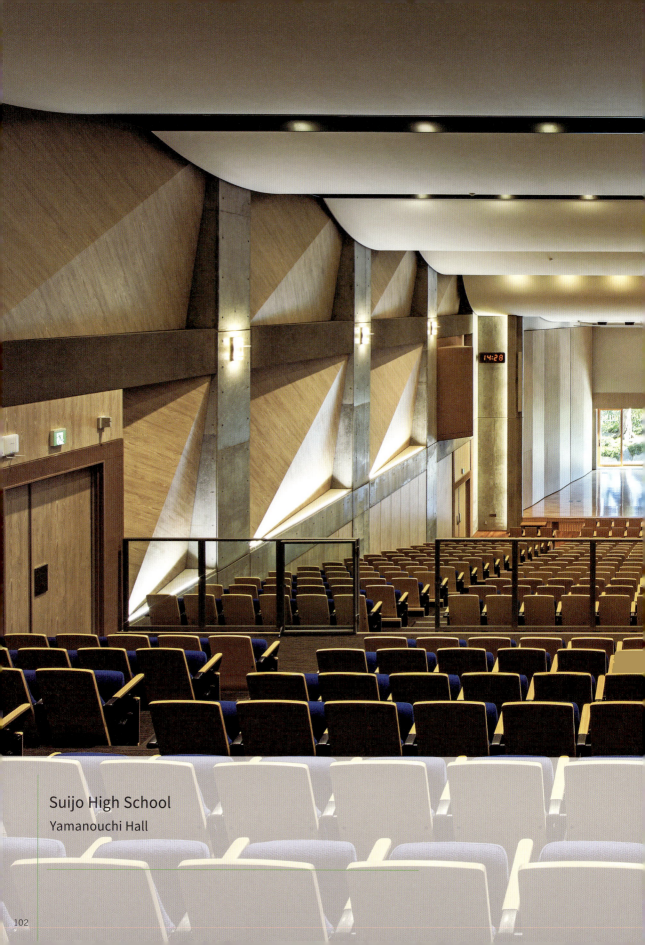

Suijo High School
Yamanouchi Hall

A new schoolhouse was constructed in 2014 to celebrate the school's 50th anniversary. In addition to the schoolhouse, the campus also contains a library, a gymnasium and a sports ground, presenting a rich variety of design including a rooftop garden and an open-air stage. Among the buildings, the Yamanouchi Hall, with its tea ceremony room set in a traditional Japanese garden, and the modern library have become symbols of the school. The hall is fitted with professional audio and lighting equipment; capable of accommodating 600, it offers a view out over the Japanese-style garden when the curtain at the rear of the stage is opened. Furthermore, when the electrically powered, retractable seating is moved into storage, the hall is transformed into an arena.

The spread of multipurpose spaces

In recent years, one of the characteristics of school architecture has been the creation of carefully thought-out, multipurpose spaces to cater for increasingly diverse curriculums and offer a richer school life. Among these are auditoriums, halls, arenas, stadiums, etc., fitted with the latest equipment, many of which are constructed to celebrate notable dates in the schools' histories, such as their 50th or 100th anniversaries.

In contrast to these major projects there are also those that employ existing facilities or make the best use of limited space by fitting retractable or moveable seating, introducing flexibility into the seating layout to create a multipurpose space. In the case of the Yamanouchi Hall, retractable seating with wall storage is used in conjunction with stacking chairs to produce a hall with tiered seating that can be moved away in a matter of minutes, converting the facility into an arena. In addition to various types of classes, it can also be utilized for a wide range of activities, such as club meetings, presentations, art appreciation, etc., allowing students of different years intermingle while also acting as a cultural center for the local neighborhood.

Location   Ibaraki
Architect Takumi Toda Architect & Associate
Completed March 2014

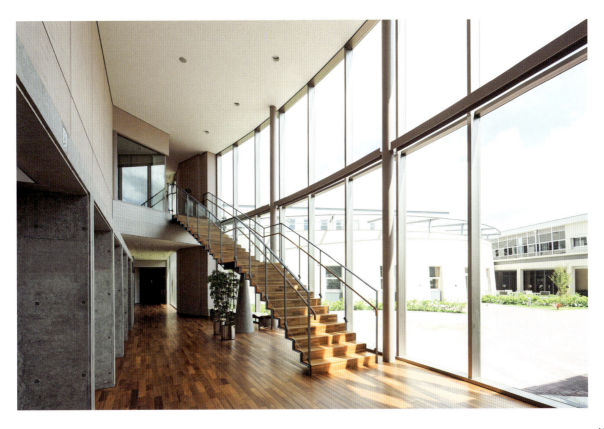

Kansai University Hokuyo Junior and Senior High School
Gymnasium

Location   Osaka
Architect   Tohata Architects & Engineers, Inc.
Completed   September 2013

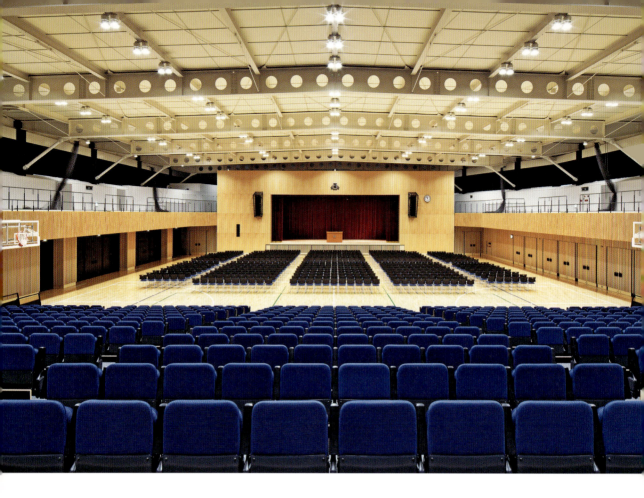

This school made a new start in 2010 as a coeducational institute combining junior and senior high schools. The newly-built gymnasium combines/merges with a sports ground that has been completely replanted with grass, offering a venue where new relationships and interactions between students of differing ages can occur. The third floor of the gymnasium contains a large hall fitted with moveable seating capable of holding 1,300. When the seating is moved into storage, it provides a huge arena containing 3 basketball courts. It also offers numerous other facilities, such as a heated, indoor swimming pool, a judo dojo, a martial arts dojo, a training gym, clubrooms, an indoor running track, etc. With the large, flat arena situated on the top floor and the other facilities all fitted into the 1st and 2nd floors, it allows the adjoining sports ground to be utilized fully, making it possible to provide both a football pitch and rugby field.

Kaichi Nihonbashi Gakuen Junior High School / Nihonbashi Jogakkan High School
Multipurpose Hall

Location   Tokyo
Architect   Tomii Architect & Associates
Completed   March 2009

A new schoolhouse was completed on the bank of Kandagawa River in the summer of 2009. This eight-story building contains an impressive range of facilities, including a rooftop sports area, which can be used for futsal or tennis, a gym, a cookery classroom, a culture room for studying tea ceremony, an IT laboratory, etc. The multipurpose hall on the 5th floor is ideal for artistic appreciation and can seat approximately 400 people. The moveable seating is electrically powered and can be stored against the wall or underneath the stage, making it possible to adjust the number of seats available. If all the seats are moved into storage, it creates an arena that can be used for club activities or sports lessons.

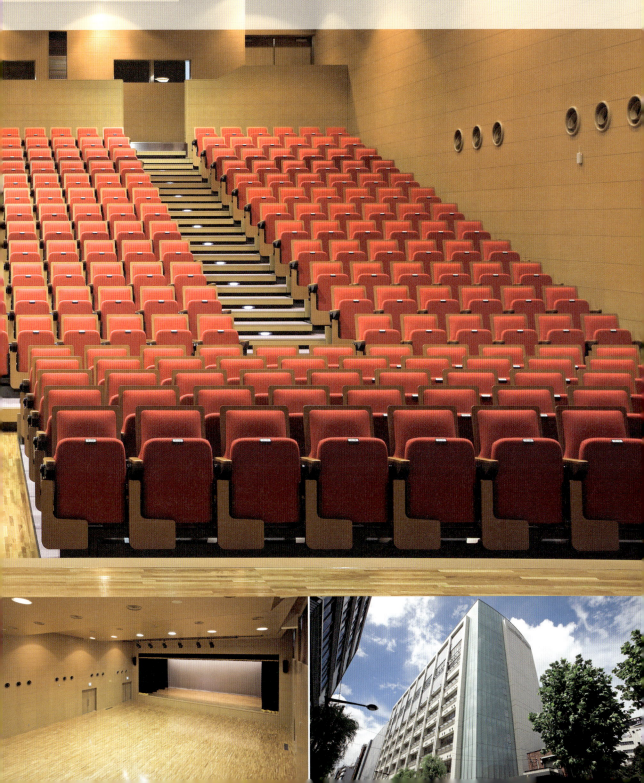

Hongo Junior and Senior High School
Auditorium

A new schoolhouse, fitted with all the latest equipment, was completed in 2014 as part of the school's 90th anniversary celebrations. This building, characterized by the unique arch that stands in the center, contains classrooms, learning space and a library, while the roof houses a baseball practice range and the basement is given over to an auditorium capable of holding 1,000 people. This full-size hall can be used for ceremonies and artistic appreciation or, if the moveable seating is stored in the walls and an electrically powered, ball protection net raised, it turns into an indoor sports facility.

Location   Tokyo
Architect   Kajima Design
Completed   January 2014

Yasuda Gakuen Junior and Senior High School
Communication Spaces

Location   Tokyo
Architect   AXS Satow Inc.
Completed   August 2013

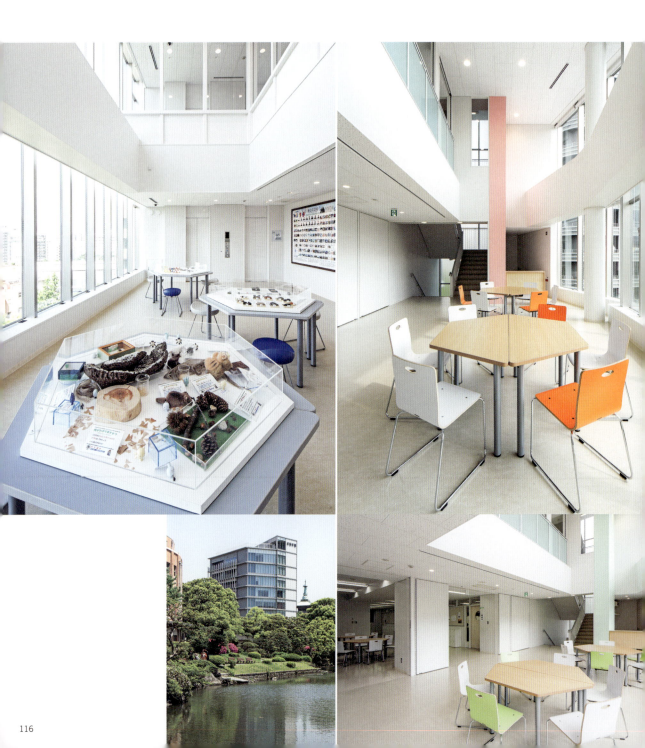

Established as a boys' school in 1923, Yasuda Gakuen boasts a history of over 90 years. In 2005 a comprehensive six-year plan was initiated to overhaul the school's educational system and in 2014 it was reborn as a coeducational school. The newly-built south building (the new junior high school building) contains a media section on the 1st floor, classrooms on the 2nd to 7th floors, a science laboratory on the 8th floor, a multipurpose room on the 9th floor and a garden on the roof that offers a vista of the Ryogoku Sumo Hall and 'Skytree' tower. High-ceilinged spaces on the 2nd, 4th and 6th floors provide communication spaces for each school year; fitted with trapezoid-shaped tables and pop-colored chairs, they present panoramic views over the Kyu-Yasuda Garden.

The American School in Japan
Multipurpose Room, Creative Arts Design Center

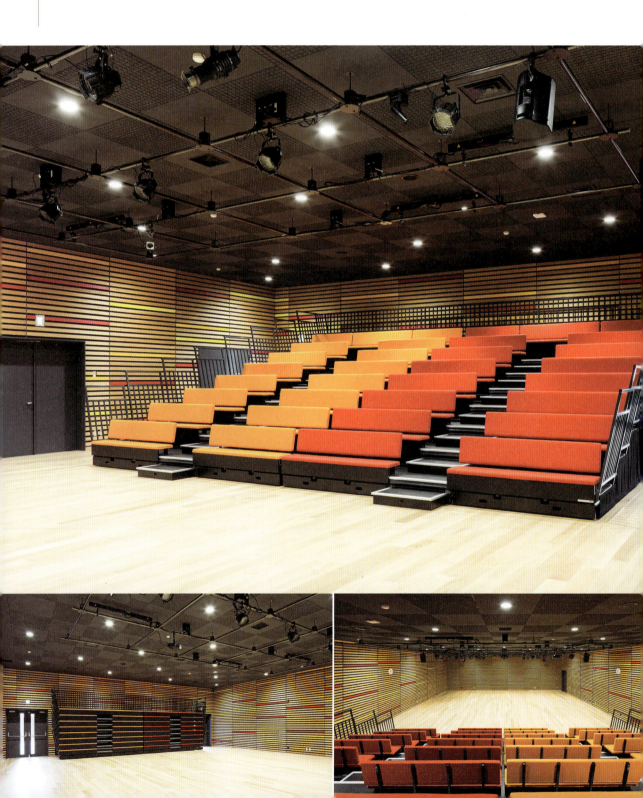

Established in 1902, this is the oldest international school in Tokyo. Situated in a rural setting next to Nogawa Park in Chofu City, it caters to approximately 1,400 students divided into 12 grades. The enlargement project, which began in 2012, resulted in the construction of a impressive entrance gateway combined with a sports facility (bottom left). The multipurpose room in the Creative Arts Design Center that was completed in 2015, contains moveable seating allowing its configuration to be altered freely. The seats are arranged in two blocks and upholstered in bright red and orange, creating a dynamic space. In addition to school events, it is also utilized for presentations and theatrical performances.

Location   Tokyo
Architect   Tange Associates
Completed   August 2015

Polaris College of Nursing
Megrez Hall

In 2013 a new educational facility appeared next to the Hoshi General Hospital in Koriyama City, Fukushima Prefecture. It was designed to provide practical technical training to raise the level of medicine and nursing while simultaneously creating a building that would heighten people's aesthetic appreciation. The symbol of the new building is the Megrez Hall that is capable of seating for 330. In addition to educational and medical lectures, it is also serves as a venue for choral concerts organized by the college, reflecting the local appreciation of music in the Koriyama district.

Upholstery Fabric

The fabric used to cover the seats is of an original design. Even though it is a plain weave, it employs a technique that creates ridges in the surface, producing an interesting texture and sheen. The dots are created using resist-dyed threads in four colors for the weft, producing an image of stars that allude to the school's name, 'Polaris' (north star). Initially the fabric was produced in two basic colors, blue and green, then actually fitted to seats of the same style in order to decide which color to use.

Location   Fukushima
Architect   Nikken Sekkei Ltd.
Completed   July 2013

Kyoto Sangyo University
Musubiwaza Hall

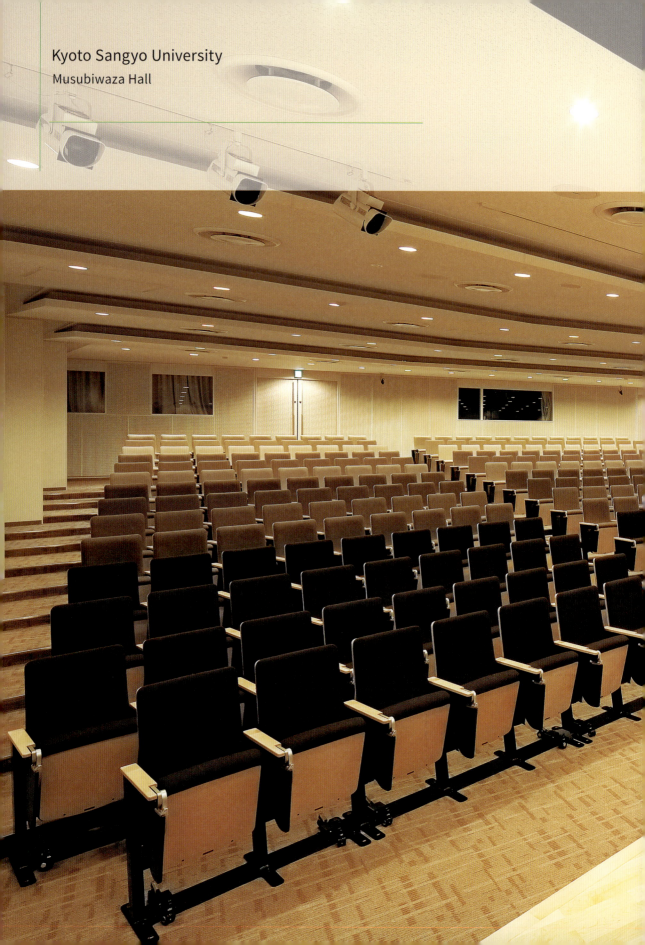

Constructed as part of the university's 50th anniversary celebrations, the Musubiwaza Hall is located in the center of the city, away from the main campus in the Kamigamo district of Kyoto, and its objective is to link the university and society through 'wisdom.' The exterior of the building comprises of grey brick, while the interior employs a lot of plain wood, combining modern architectural design with the traditional image of Kyoto. Containing seating for 418, the front two rows employ moveable seating, allowing changes to be made according to the objective of the event being held. The fabric used in the upholstery produces a gradation of color, adding feeling of depth to this building that has a rather low ceiling.

Location   Kyoto
Architect Takenaka Corporation
Completed February 2012

Kawasaki Junior and Senior High School
Auditorium

Location   Kanagawa
Architect Azusa Sekkei Co., ltd.
Completed August 2014

This institute opened in 2014 as the first municipal school in Kawasaki City to combine junior and senior high school education. It has received a lot of attention due to the fact that it offers both daytime and nighttime courses, allowing people of all ages to study. Utilizing the school buildings that used to house the Kawasaki Senior High School, it was completely renovated and fitted with an indoor swimming pool, tennis courts, arena, etc., to provide a comprehensive sports facility, while on the cultural front a large auditorium capable of holding 500 was also established as an annex. All the seats are fitted with a table in the backrest allowing them to be used for lectures in addition to school events.

Toyama Chubu High School
Shisei Hall

Location Toyama
Architect Fukumi Architect & Associates Co., Ltd.
Completed March 2014

Established in 1920, Toyama Chubu High School has already celebrated its 96th anniversary and is one of the oldest schools in the prefecture. The new school building, which was completed in 2014, is constructed around an inner court creating a cloister. The building grows taller from south to north capturing as much sunlight as possible while simultaneously ensuring good ventilation. The Shisei Hall is a multipurpose facility with a seating capacity of 315 (including moveable seating) and serves as a symbol of the school.

Kyushu High School Affiliated
with Kyushu Sangyo University
Kyushu Community Hall

As part of the school's 50th anniversary celebrations in 2013, a new building was constructed on the site of the old indoor swimming pool, containing a community hall, academic plaza (a space for carrying out art and science club activities), and an art library (a space for reading and art exhibitions), providing a new venue for cultural exchange. The hall is capable of seating 612, using a combination of fixed seating and stacking chairs, allowing it to be used for academic activities. Glass windows are fitted into the exterior walls, interior walls and ceilings, filling the space with light.

Location   Fukuoka
Architect   Kazumi Kudo + Hiroshi Horiba,
             Coelacanth K&H
Completed   November 2013

Shoshikan High School
Audiovisual Hall

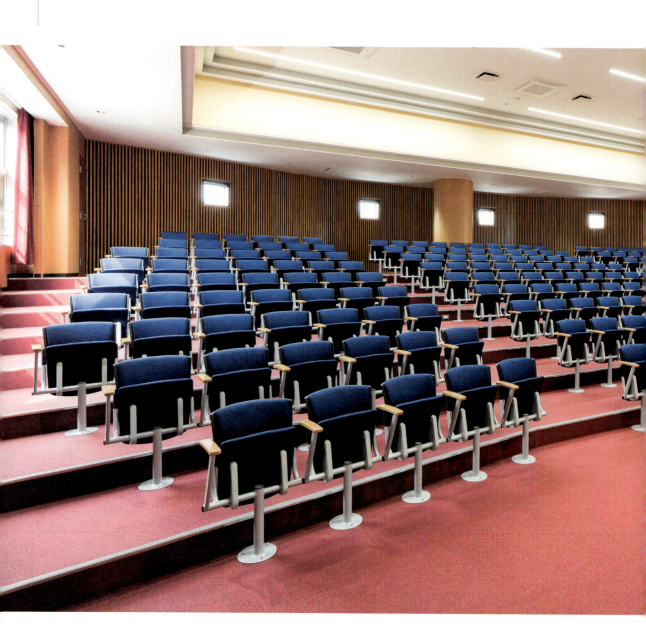

In 2016, three new, three-story buildings were constructed to celebrate the school's centenary in 2016: the new Administrative Building, the Center Hall, and the Classroom Building. The atrium that serves as the entrance hall of the administrative building presents a unique design. The Center Hall, which stands in the inner court, has an Audiovisual Hall installed on the 3rd floor with a tiered structure allowing a view over all the seats from the rostrum. It contains 206 fold-down seats with a modern appearance, each mounted on a single leg and fitted with a single armrest. The rostrum is equipped with a large screen allowing it to be used for lectures, cultural exchange, and classes presented by visiting alumni, providing a stimulating, intellectual space.

Location   Kagoshima
Architect   Eto Nakayama Sekkei Co., Ltd.
Completed   July 2015

Nakano Junior and Senior High School Attached to Meiji University
Sakurayama Hall

This is the only boy's school affiliated with Meiji University. The school grounds face onto a road which is planted with cherry trees for approximately 150 meters and affectionately known by the local people as 'Sakurayama Road.' In 2009, as the school approached its 80th anniversary, it was decided to commemorate this fact by replacing the school buildings. The objective was to improve the educational environment while simultaneously upgrading its function as a emergency evacuation center. Completed in 2016, the Sakurayama Hall was designed to serve as a multipurpose space and to this end, it employs flat-floor type seating that folds electronically, allowing it to be stored beneath the rear seats. The walls and floor employ the same shades of blue as the upholstery, creating an active and lively atmosphere.

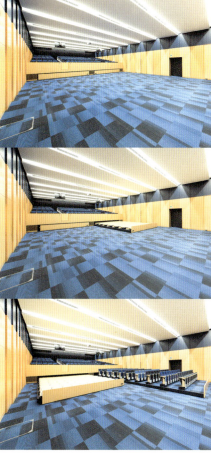

Location   Tokyo
Architect Nikken Sekkei Ltd.
Completed March 2016

Hokkaido Otani Muroran High School
Auditorium

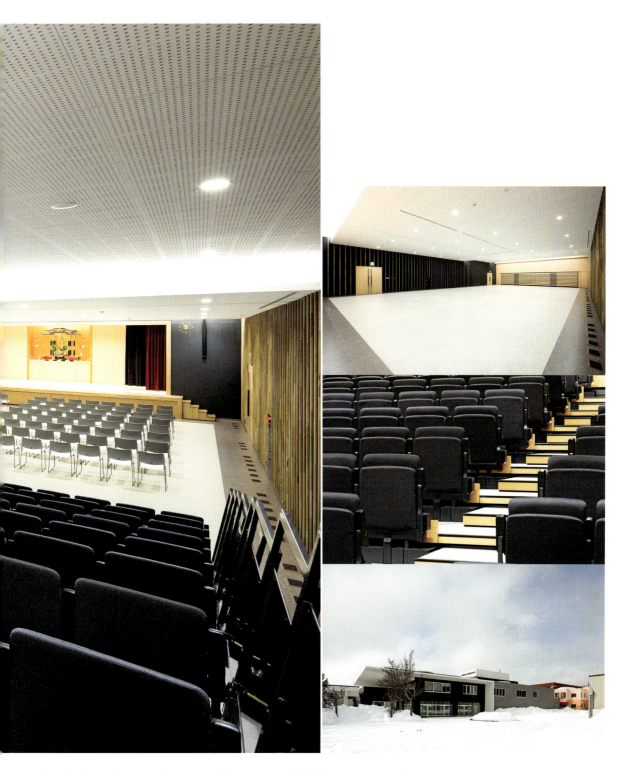

This school was formed in the spring of 2012 as a result of the integration of two existing schools. Coincident with the merging of the schools, a plan was drawn up to replace the old school buildings and in 2015, a new auditorium was completed. The seating in the front of the hall utilizes stacking chairs while the rear is taken up with moveable spectator seating, making a variety of layouts possible. By altering the number of seats used and adding dividers, it is possible to use it as either a hall capable of seating a maximum of 500, or alternatively as an open space. In 2016 it served as the venue for a coming-of-age ceremony for members of the alumni.

Location   Hokkaido
Architect   Nihon Sekkei Inc.
Completed   November 2014

Nichinan Gakuen Junior and Senior High School
Portsmouth Hall

Nichinan City in Miyazaki Prefecture was the birthplace of Jutaro Komura, the Foreign Minister who signed the Portsmouth Treaty in 1905. As a result, there is a strong connection between this school and Portsmouth high school in New Hampshire, U.S.A., with homestay programs being carried out by both schools. A new school building was completed in 2014, with the opening ceremony being held on September 5, the same day that the Portsmouth Treaty was signed, and the school echoed to the sound of a bell donated by Nichinan's sister city, Portsmouth, to celebrate the occasion. The Portsmouth Hall on the 2nd floor is quite small, capable of seating only 171, but great attention was paid to its acoustics and it is a serious facility, used mainly for musical recitals and practice by the choral club.

Location Miyazaki
Architect Matsuo Construction Co., Ltd.
          Shiba Sekkei
Completed July 2014

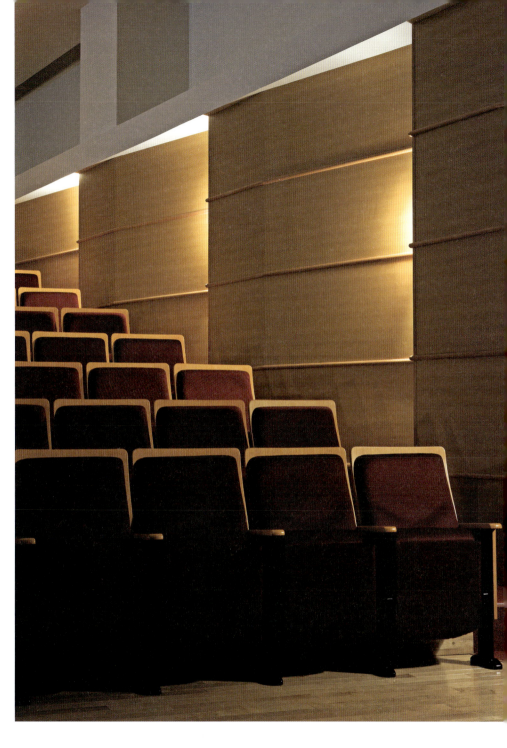

Tamagawa University
Drama Studio

Location	Tokyo
Architect	Miura-Nishino Sekkei
Completed	April 1976

This facility was refurbished in 2010 to provide a performance space for students studying at the College of Arts. The existing seating, which could be stored in the walls, was changed from bench type to individual chairs and a crimson tone, that looks most attractive under the stage lighting, was selected for the upholstery. The unusual polygonal shape of the studio can be utilized to create numerous combinations of moveable seating and stacking chairs to produce a wide variety of layouts and creating a theater in which the stage and seating merge together to generate a rich ambiance.

Aoyama Gakuin Elementary School
Yoneyama Memorial Chapel

Location   Tokyo
Architect   Shimizu Corporation
Completed   March 2007

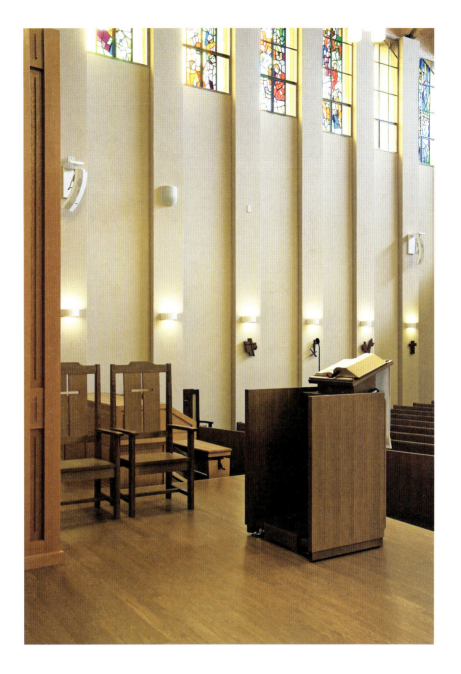

Standing on the site of a mansion that once belonged to Prince Komatsu-no-Miya, the campus covers 10,000 square meters and includes the traditional Japanese garden dating from when it was a private domicile. Work began on replacing the school buildings in 2004 and the first to be completed was the 'Upper Grades Building,' which caters for the 5th and 6th graders, boasting a rooftop garden and a heated, indoor swimming pool in the basement. The 'Lower and Middle Grades Building' for the 1st through 4th graders, which includes an open dining hall, was completed next, followed by the new chapel. Dedicated in 2007, this chapel is a spacious building, with a ceiling more than 13 meters tall, it contains 16 stained-glass windows by the Western-style artist, Tadao Tanaka (1903-95) and a 'Coalition Cross,' consisting of multiple crosses in increasing sizes, stands on the altar. The pipe organ is made by Germany's Rudolf von Beckerath company, and has a total of 2,091 pipes. The classic pews are made of oak and provide seating for 950, allowing the entire elementary school to come together and interact through religion.

152	Waseda University	Building No. 3
160	Tokyo University of Science	Library Hall
164	Nakamura Gakuen Girl's Junior and Senior High School	Auditorium, Cooking Demonstration Hall
168	Seiko Gakuin Junior and Senior High School| Auditorium
172	Tamagawa University	University Hall 2014
176	Showa Women's University	Cosmos Hall
180	Tokyo Institute of Technology	Lecture Theater [Restoration]
184	Hokkaido University	Multi-purpose Hall
186	Okinawa Institute of Science and Technology Graduate University (OIST)	Auditorium
190	Tokyo University of Agriculture	Nodai Academia Center Yokoi Hall
192	Meiji University	Global Hall
196	Aichi Gakuin University	Castle Hall
200	Kogakuin University	Hachioji Campus
202	Doshisha University	Ryoshinkan Building
206	University of Toyama	Nichiiko Auditorium
208	Kitasato University	Towada Campus
210	Obihiro University of Agriculture and Veterinary Medicine	Clinical Lecture Room
212	Jissen Gakuen Junior and Senior High School	Freedom Hall
216	Makuhari Junior and Senior High School	Lecture Hall
218	Mita International School
220	Senzoku Gakuen College of Music	Silver Mountain
224	Aoyama Gakuin University	Building A Arena
226	Nihon University	Sports Hall Arena
230	Nippon Sport Science University	Main Arena
232	Osaka Toin Junior and Senior High School	Toin Arena